THE DIVINE PRINCIPLE VS. THE HOLY BIBLE

A Biblical Response to Unification Church Teachings

Susan Puzio

Copyright Page

Scripture quotations are taken from the King James Version of the Bible.

Quotations from *Exposition of the Divine Principle* (1996 English edition) are reproduced for purposes of theological analysis, documentation, and critical commentary. All such quotations remain the property of their respective copyright holders.

This publication is an independent theological work. It is not affiliated with, endorsed by, authorized by, or sponsored by the Family Federation for World Peace and Unification, the Unification Church, the Universal Peace Federation, or any related organization. All organizational names are used for identification and descriptive purposes only.

ISBN: 978-1-882970-05-6

First Edition

Printed in the United States of America

For permissions, media inquiries, or correspondence:
Susan Puzio
[susan@propheticnews.com]
[propheticnews.com]

TABLE OF CONTENTS

📓 PREFACE — Methodology, Sources, and Purpose

This book is written to address a specific and critical central question.

Can the theology presented in *Exposition of the Divine Principle* be reconciled with the teachings of Jesus Christ and the Holy Scriptures as preserved in the King James version of the Bible? Its purpose is theological doctrinal analysis and documented examination and comparison.

Methodology

The method used throughout this book is straightforward and verifiable:

1. Direct quotations from the *Divine Principle*: All citations of Unification theology are taken from the publicly available 1996 edition of *Exposition of the Divine Principle*, accessible at: https://www.unification.net/dp96/

Citations are referenced by part, chapter, and section, allowing readers to verify the original context directly from the source.

Note on editions:
This work cites the 1996 English edition of *Exposition of the Divine Principle* (HSA-UWC). While the doctrinal content of that edition remains consistent, minor differences in layout, pagination, and digital formatting may appear across printings and online versions. For this reason, references are provided by part, chapter, and section rather than by page number.

2. Direct quotations from Scripture:
   All biblical citations are taken from the King James version of the Bible. Doctrinal comparisons rest on the text itself.

3. Side-by-side doctrinal comparison:
   Claims made in the *Divine Principle* are examined alongside relevant biblical passages. The analysis asks whether the two teachings can coexist without contradiction.

4. No reliance on secondary or unfriendly sources. This work does not depend on critics, journalists, or former members. The *Divine Principle* is allowed to speak for itself, and Scripture is allowed to respond for itself.

Scope and Limits

This book focuses on:

- The person and work of Jesus Christ
- The meaning and sufficiency of the cross
- Salvation, grace, and redemption
- Authority and revelation
- Is there a theological necessity for additional messianic figures?

It does not attempt to catalog every historical event or organizational development within the Unification movement. Where public figures, pastors, artists, or political leaders are mentioned, the documentation is limited strictly to public participation at events.

Purpose

The goal of this book is not just persuasion by rhetoric, but clarity and openness through comparison.

Readers are encouraged to:

- Review the *Divine Principle* only for comparison and consult it directly for exact quotations.
- Read Scripture directly and then compare both carefully.

The truth wins (John 8:32): "And ye shall know the truth, and the truth shall make you free."

As Scripture instructs:

> "Prove all things; hold fast that which is good."
> — 1 Thessalonians 5:21

Note to the reader:

True Christian faith stands on the sufficiency of Jesus Christ, who provides everything that we need, and on the authority of Scripture. This belief is rooted in the doctrine of *sola scriptura*, which asserts that the Bible alone is the inspired and infallible Word of God, providing all necessary guidance for life and godliness. Any teaching that alters this cannot be accepted as true Christianity. We ask you to examine this manuscript carefully and to know that our heart is for you to know true peace and true joy, only found in accepting Christ Jesus as Lord.

This book is offered in that spirit.

CHAPTER ONE — Another Jesus, Another Gospel

The Divine Principle *Examined Against Scripture*

---

1. Introduction: The Priority of Scripture in Christian Doctrine

The book of Corinthians warns the early church about doctrinal deception.

> "But I fear, lest by any means, as the serpent beguiled Eve through his subtilty, so your minds should be corrupted from the simplicity that is in Christ."
> — 2 Corinthians 11:3

The concern here is that of preaching **another Jesus**, another gospel, and another spirit. Paul explicitly identified this pattern as a primary threat to the integrity of Christian faith.

> "For if he that cometh preacheth another Jesus, whom we have not preached, or *if* ye receive another spirit,

> which ye have not received, or another gospel, which ye have not accepted, ye might well bear with *him*."
> — 2 Corinthians 11:4

> "For nothing is secret, that shall not be made manifest: neither any thing hid, that shall not be known and come abroad."

— Luke 8:17

The New Testament consistently holds the gospel of Jesus Christ as **complete and sufficient**, not expandable or replaceable.

---

2. *Divine Principle's* Christology and Its Claims

Within the *Divine Principle* text — as presented in the 1996 Exposition — the Christology section (*DP*96, Part I, Chapter 7, Christology) frames critical questions concerning the identity and mission of Jesus, the Trinity, and rebirth. The *DP*96 text states:

> "For fallen people who seek salvation… the key… is to understand the original value of human beings."
> — *DP*96, Part I, Chapter 7, Christology
> tparents.org

The focus here is **not first on the person of Christ**, but on *human potential and original value*. The Christology section proceeds directly into cultural and metaphysical frameworks. Metaphysical here means "metaphysics illuminates hidden assumptions."

Importantly — and this is central to the theological contrast — the *Divine Principle* asserts that **Jesus' mission remained partial and incomplete** because humanity failed to fulfill required conditions.

In *DP*96, the cross and Jesus' death are framed within a larger providential process: *Jesus did not complete restoration, and resurrection (as part of the providence of restoration) remains incomplete until the Second Advent.* For example:

> "Due to the crucifixion of Jesus, resurrection was left incomplete, and its completion has been delayed until the time of His return."
> — *DP*96, Part II, Chapter 5, Section 2.2.3 (Providence of Resurrection) tparents.org

In this teaching, even resurrection — a central component of Christian faith — is held to be **unfinished without another coming**.

---

3. Scripture on the Sufficiency and Finality of Christ's Work

The Bible consistently declares that **Christ's work on the cross was complete and final**. Jesus said:

> "It is finished."
> — John 19:30

The Greek term *tetelestai* signifies *completion*, not deficiency. Tetelestai means "it is finished," which are known as Jesus' last words on the cross. It signifies completion and the fulfillment of the scriptures, indicating that the work of redemption was accomplished.

The author of Hebrews underscores this sufficiency:

> "By one offering he hath perfected for ever them that are sanctified."
> — Hebrews 10:14

Here the verb *perfected* means brought to completion. There is no hint that more work remains.

Peter affirms the singularity of Christ's sacrifice:

> "Who his own self bare our sins in his own body on the tree."
> — 1 Peter 2:24

Christ's death is not a preliminary stage to be followed later by physical or lineage restoration.

---

4. Another Gospel Requires Another Christ

According to the *Divine Principle*, because the intended mission of Christ was not completed — especially in terms of physical or familial restoration — **another messianic figure or return is required**.

> "Christ must come again in flesh in order… to complete the providence of restoration."
> — DP96, Part I, Chapter 7, Section 4

This theological position directly diverges from New Testament teaching. The author of Hebrews identifies Christ's return as **not to complete atonement**, but salvation was already won at the cross.

> "So Christ was once offered to bear the sins of many; and unto them that look for him shall he appear the second time without sin unto salvation."
> — Hebrews 9:28

The return of Christ is not described as a **second Messiah** or a *completer* of an unfinished mission. It is the **same** Savior, Jesus Christ:

> "Wherefore he is able also to save them to the uttermost that come unto God by him, seeing he ever liveth to make

intercession for them."
— Hebrews 7:25

This language of sufficiency, completeness, and finality stands in contrast to a theology that assigns completion to another future figure.

---

5. Theological and Exegetical Implications (explanatory)

The *Divine Principle* redistributes emphasis from *Christ's unique and sufficient atonement* to a **historical process that requires human conditions** and a future completion through additional messianic action.

The *DP*96 vision of resurrection and restoration involves eras and stages, where spiritual restoration precedes physical and completion-stage resurrection is deferred. Scripture, however, proclaims that:

- Salvation is **received by faith alone** — not by stages. (Ephesians 2:8–9)

- Christ's death is **once for all** — not pending completion. (Hebrews 10:10)
- Resurrection-"But now is Christ risen from the dead, *and* become the firstfruits of them that slept." (1 Corinthians 15:20)

The *Divine Principle's* layered providential model shifts the emphasis from the sufficiency of Christ's completed work to an ongoing historical process that requires future fulfillment.

---

6. Conclusion: Another Jesus, Another Gospel

Paul's criterion for testing teaching is clear:

> "As we said before, so say I now again, If any man preach any other gospel unto you than that ye have received, let him be accursed."
>
> — Galatians 1:9

Where Christ's atoning work is depicted as unfinished, another redeemer is implied. Where salvation is portrayed as partial, another gospel is present.

The *Divine Principle* asserts that Jesus *did not complete* the providence of restoration, that resurrection remains incomplete until a future return, and that human conditions and eras must be satisfied in partnership with divine work. These teachings fundamentally alter the biblical gospel, not merely by adding nuance or suggestion but by totally redefining completion, resurrection, and Messiahship.

CHAPTER TWO — The Cross Was Not Plan B

Divine Principle *Teaching Compared with Scripture*

---

1. Introduction: Why the Meaning of the Cross Is Decisive

The finished work at the cross stands at the center of Christianity. If the meaning of the cross is altered, true Christianity itself is altered.

> "For I determined not to know any thing among you, save Jesus Christ, and him crucified.
> — 1 Corinthians 2:2

Any theology that reinterprets the purpose, necessity, or outcome of the cross must therefore be tested with the utmost seriousness and rejected.

---

2. The *Divine Principle* Claim: The Cross Was Not God's Original Will

The *Divine Principle* explicitly teaches that the crucifixion of Jesus was **not** the fulfillment of God's original plan. Instead, it is presented as a secondary outcome necessitated by human failure.

The *Divine Principle* teaches that had the Jewish people believed in Jesus, the crucifixion would not have occurred (Part I, Chapter 4, Section *1.6*).

This statement is foundational. It establishes the cross as **avoidable**, not necessary, and frames it as a deviation from God's intent rather than the execution of divine purpose.

The *Divine Principle* continues:

> "Jesus' crucifixion brought spiritual salvation alone."
> — *DP*96, Part I, Chapter 4, Section 1

According to this framework, the cross didn't complete redemption but merely initiated a partial, spiritual phase of restoration. DP has a very different view of "spiritual salvation."

---

3. Scripture: The Cross as the Foreordained Will of God

Scripture directly contradicts this portrayal. The New Testament presents the crucifixion as both foreknown and foreordained by God.

Peter declares at Pentecost:

> "Him, being delivered by the determinate counsel and foreknowledge of God, ye have taken, and by wicked hands have crucified and slain."
> — Acts 2:23

The phrase *determinate counsel* doesn't allow for contingency, backup, or surprise. The cross wasn't a temporary provisional response to failure.

The prophet Isaiah speaks with equal clarity:

> "Yet it pleased the LORD to bruise him; he hath put him to grief: when thou shalt make his soul an offering for sin, he shall see his seed, he shall prolong his days, and the pleasure of the LORD

> shall prosper in his hand."
> — Isaiah 53:10

The suffering and death of the Messiah aren't attributed to human error, misjudgment, or miscalculation, but to divine intention.

---

4. Jesus' Own Testimony About His Death

Jesus Himself repeatedly affirmed that His death was necessary, not avoidable.

> "And he began to teach them, that the Son of man must suffer many things, and be rejected of the elders, and of the chief priests, and scribes, and be killed, and after three days rise again."
> — Mark 8:31

The use of *must* (*dei* in Greek) signifies divine necessity.

It wasn't murder. Jesus said:

> "As the Father knoweth me, even so know I the Father: and I lay down my life for the sheep. And other sheep I

> have, which are not of this fold: them also I must bring, and they shall hear my voice; and there shall be one-fold, and one shepherd. Therefore doth my Father love me, because I lay down my life, that I might take it again. **No man taketh it from me, but I lay it down of myself. I have power to lay it down, and I have power to take it again. This commandment have I received of my Father.**"
>
> — John 10:15-18

After His resurrection, Jesus rebuked His disciples for failing to understand this:

> "Ought not Christ to have suffered these things, and to enter into his glory?"
>
> — Luke 24:26

The question presumes a scriptural inevitability. Jesus doesn't portray the cross as an unfortunate detour.

5. The *Divine Principle*'s Division of Salvation

A critical theological divergence appears in the *Divine Principle*'s division of salvation into **spiritual** and **physical** components.

*DP*96 states:

> "Through the crucifixion, Jesus accomplished spiritual salvation, but the purpose of physical salvation was left unfulfilled."
> — *DP*96, Part I, Chapter 7, Section 3

This framework implies that:

- Sin is not fully dealt with at the cross
- Restoration must continue historically
- A future messianic figure is required to complete what Jesus began

Scripture doesn't recognize such a division.

---

6. Scripture: Salvation as Complete and Undivided

The New Testament consistently presents salvation as **total**, not partial.

> "Who his own self bare our sins in his own body on the tree."
> — 1 Peter 2:24

Sin isn't described as partially forgiven.

Paul writes:

> "And you, being dead in your sins… hath he quickened together with him, having forgiven you all trespasses."
> — Colossians 2:13

"All trespasses" leaves no remainder.

The author of Hebrews emphasizes finality:

> "By the which will we are sanctified through the offering of the body of Jesus Christ once for all."
>
> — Hebrews 10:10

---

7. The Consequence of Denying the Finality of the Cross

When the cross is redefined as insufficient, additional strange doctrines inevitably follow. The *Divine Principle* does so by:

- introducing historical restoration stages
- emphasizing human responsibility and indemnity
- anticipating a future central figure to complete salvation

Paul warned precisely against this pattern:

> "I do not frustrate the grace of God: for if righteousness come by the law, then Christ is dead in vain."
> — Galatians 2:21

If something essential remains unfinished, grace is no longer grace.

---

8. The Cross in Biblical Preaching

The New Testament never treated the cross as incomplete.

> "For the preaching of the cross is to them that perish foolishness; but unto us which are saved it is the power of God."
> — 1 Corinthians 1:18

The cross isn't a temporary measure; it's the power of God unto salvation.

---

9. Conclusion: The Cross Was the Plan

The *Divine Principle* teaches that Jesus didn't complete the full original purpose of His messianic mission. Scripture teaches that the cross occurred because God's foreordained plan succeeded.

> "For I delivered unto you first of all that which I also received, how that Christ died for our sins according to the scriptures;"
> — 1 Corinthians 15:3

There is no biblical category for a "Plan B" atonement.

If the cross isn't sufficient, another gospel would follow.

Conclusion

By portraying the crucifixion as avoidable, partial, and incomplete, the *Divine Principle* fundamentally departs from biblical Christianity. Scripture consistently affirms that the cross was necessary, foreordained, and fully effective.

The cross was not Plan B. It was the plan, and Jesus yet again affirmed it at the time of His arrest.

> "Thinkest thou that I cannot now pray to my Father, and he shall presently give me more than twelve legions of angels? But how then shall the scriptures be fulfilled, that thus it must be?"
>
> — Matthew 26:53-54

CHAPTER THREE — Another Gospel Requires Another Messiah

Why an Incomplete Christ Necessitates a Replacement Christ

---

1. Introduction: The Logic of Substitution

True Christian doctrine cannot be rearranged without distortion and corruption as a consequence. When one doctrine is altered, others must change to compensate. This is especially true of Christology. If Jesus Christ didn't complete His mission, then some can say that their version of Christianity must logically await another figure to finish what remains undone.

1 Timothy identifies this danger explicitly:

> "For there is one God, and one mediator between God and men, the man Christ Jesus."
> — 1 Timothy 2:5

True biblical Christianity stands on the exclusivity and sufficiency of Christ as Mediator and Savior. There is no allowance for successors, supplements, or corrective Messiahs.

---

2. The *Divine Principle* Claim: The Messiah's Mission Was Left Unfinished

The *Divine Principle* directly teaches that Jesus' mission was incomplete and therefore requires a future fulfillment.

*DP*96 states:

> "Jesus did not accomplish the purpose of the Messiah. Hence Christ must come again."
> — *Exposition of the Divine Principle* (1996), Part I, Chapter 7, Section 4 ("The Second Advent of the Messiah")

This assertion is foundational. The necessity of the Second Advent, as defined in the *Divine Principle*, is not merely Christ's return, but **the completion of an unfulfilled messianic task**.

The text continues:

> "The mission of the Second Advent is to complete the purpose of creation

> which Jesus did not fulfill."
> — *DP*96, Part I, Chapter 7, Section 4

Here the Second Advent isn't portrayed as the return of Jesus and His victory over sin and death and His role as the exalted Savior who returns to judge and restore all things, but as the arrival of a figure who must accomplish what Jesus failed to complete.

---

3. Scripture: The Second Coming Is Not the Arrival of a Successor

The New Testament presents the return of Jesus as the triumphant King of Kings and Lord of Lords.

In Revelation 19:11, it states,

> "And I saw heaven opened, and behold a white horse; and he that sat upon him was called Faithful and True, and in righteousness he doth judge and make war."

The author of Hebrews states:

> "So Christ was once offered to bear the sins of many; and unto them that look for him shall he appear the second time without sin unto salvation."
> — Hebrews 9:28

Paul reinforces this:

> "Christ being raised from the dead dieth no more; death hath no more dominion over him."
> — Romans 6:9

If Christ doesn't die again, He doesn't atone again. There is no remaining redemptive deficiency to be addressed by another figure.

---

4. The *Divine Principle*'s Reinterpretation of the Second Advent

The *Divine Principle* redefines the Second Advent away from bodily return and judgment toward **mission completion through another human figure**.

*DP*96 teaches:

> "The Lord of the Second Advent must be born on earth as a man, just as Jesus was."
> — *DP*96, Part I, Chapter 7, Section 4

This claim introduces a **second messianic individual** distinct from Jesus of Nazareth, and the identity of Christ is functionally replaced.

Scripture explicitly rejects this possibility.

---

5. Scripture: The Identity of Christ Is Non-Transferable

Jesus didn't describe His return as the appearance of another individual, but as **His own visible, personal return**.

> "And then shall they see the Son of man coming in the clouds with great power and glory."
> — Mark 13:26

Scripture affirmed this at the ascension:

> "This same Jesus, which is taken up from you into heaven, shall so come in

> like manner as ye have seen him go into heaven."
> — Acts 1:11

There is no scriptural allowance for a different man, born later, assuming Christ's messianic role.

---

6. Mediation Cannot Be Shared or Inherited

The *Divine Principle* framework ultimately requires an additional mediator to complete restoration. Scripture categorically forbids this.

> "Neither is there salvation in any other: for there is none other name under heaven given among men, whereby we must be saved."
> — Acts 4:12

Christ's priesthood is permanent:

> "But this man, because he continueth ever, hath an unchangeable priesthood."
> — Hebrews 7:24

The Greek term *aparabatos* ("unchangeable") means **non-transferable**. Christ's mediating role cannot be passed to another. It is permanent.

---

7. The Problem of a Successor Messiah

Once the idea of an unfinished Christ is accepted, theological consequences multiply:

- A **new revelator** is required
- A **new interpretive authority** emerges
- Scripture becomes **insufficient without explanation**
- Loyalty shifts from Christ to the new central figure

Paul warned of this exact trajectory:

> "For I know this, that after my departing shall grievous wolves enter in among you, not sparing the flock.
> Also of your own selves shall men arise, speaking perverse things, to draw away disciples after them."
> — Acts 20:29–30

The issue is not merely doctrinal error, but **discipleship displacement** away from the real Jesus.

---

8. The Sufficiency of Christ According to Scripture

The New Testament repeatedly emphasizes the totality of Christ's saving work.

> "Wherefore he is able also to save them to the uttermost that come unto God by him, seeing he ever liveth to make intercession for them."
> — Hebrews 7:25

"To the uttermost" (*pantelēs*) means **completely, perfectly, without remainder**.

Paul affirms:

> "For in him dwelleth all the fulness of the Godhead bodily.
> And ye are complete in him, which is the head of all principality and power."
> — Colossians 2:9–10

Believers are already complete in Christ. No additional Messiah is needed or anticipated.

---

9. Conclusion: A Different Messiah Produces a Different Gospel

The *Divine Principle* teaches that Jesus didn't complete the messianic mission and that another figure must do so. Scripture teaches that Jesus Christ completed our redemption once for all and will return in glory, and in total victory.

Paul's warning remains decisive:

> "But though we, or an angel from heaven, preach any other gospel unto you than that which we have preached unto you, let him be accursed."
> — Galatians 1:8

A gospel that requires another Messiah isn't true Christianity refined; it's true Christianity replaced.

Conclusion

The *Divine Principle*'s necessity for a Second Advent figure arises directly from its denial of Christ's sufficiency. Scripture allows no such denial. Christ alone is Savior, Mediator, and Messiah — yesterday, today, and forever.

> "Jesus Christ the same yesterday, and today, and for ever."
> — Hebrews 13:8

Chapter Four- From Visionary to "Lord of the Second Advent"

The Development of Sun Myung Moon's Authority

---

1. Introduction: How Authority Is Constructed

Every religious movement must answer a fundamental question: **By what authority does it speak?** In biblical Christianity, authority flows from God revealing Himself in Scripture and in Jesus Christ and is centered in His finished work.

> "Search the scriptures; for in them ye think ye have eternal life: and they are they which testify of me."
> — John 5:39

Movements that displace Scripture as the final authority will elevate another source—often a founder whose experiences, interpretations, or revelations become decisive.

The *Divine Principle* presents such a shift.

---

2. The Foundational Vision Claim

Unification teaching universally rests upon the claim that Sun Myung Moon received a private revelation from Jesus as a young man, assigning him a mission.

This framework is essential, because without a divine commission, Moon's theological authority collapses.

Scripture provides a clear warning regarding private revelations that introduce new doctrine:

> "Beloved, believe not every spirit, but
> try the spirits whether they are of God."
> — 1 John 4:1

The standard of testing is **the Word of God**, not experiences.

---

3. The Divine Principle's Theology of Mission Transfer

The *Divine Principle* teaches that Jesus' failure to complete restoration necessitated a continuation of the messianic mission.

*DP*96 states:

> "Jesus could not fulfill the ideal of the Messiah during his lifetime. Therefore, the providence of restoration must be completed through the Second Advent."
> — *Exposition of the Divine Principle* (1996), Part I, Chapter 7, Section 4

This doctrine establishes the **conceptual vacancy** into which Sun Myung Moon's authority would later be placed.

The Messiah's role, according to *DP*96, is transferable—not final.

---

4. Central Figure

When it is claimed that Scripture requires the Divine Principle for its correct interpretation, authority shifts to the one who defines that Principle. Scripture warns against this dynamic:

> "Beware lest any man spoil you through philosophy and vain deceit, after the

> tradition of men."
> — Colossians 2:8

---

5. The Divine Principle's Concept of "True Parents"

The *Divine Principle* teaches that restoration requires perfected human parents to reverse the fall.

*DP*96 explains:

> "The mission of the Messiah is to restore the original position of the first human ancestors."
> — *DP*96, Part I, Chapter 7, Section 1

This role goes beyond teaching or leadership. The Messiah must restore lineage.

Scripture categorically rejects lineage-based salvation.

> "Which were born, not of blood, nor of the will of the flesh, nor of the will of man, but of God."
> — John 1:13

Salvation is spiritual rebirth, not genealogical correction.

---

6. Scripture: Christ Alone Redeems Humanity

The New Testament identifies Jesus—not a future couple—as the **Second Adam**.

> "The first man Adam was made a living soul; the last Adam was made a quickening spirit."
> — 1 Corinthians 15:45

There is no biblical category for a *third* Adam or a corrective pair.

Note the word "last." Jesus Christ redeemed us not through marriage or lineage, but through His death, burial, and resurrection:

> "For as in Adam all die, even so in Christ shall all be made alive."
> — 1 Corinthians 15:22

---

7. The Gradual Emergence of Messianic Identity

Once the theological framework is established—unfinished Jesus, transferable mission, lineage restoration—the elevation of Sun Myung Moon becomes logically inevitable.

Jesus warned against such developments:

> "Then if any man shall say unto you, Lo, here is Christ, or there; believe it not. For there shall arise false Christs, and false prophets, and shall shew great signs and wonders; insomuch that, if it were possible, they shall deceive the very elect."
> — Matthew 24:23-24

---

8. The Authority Test: Scripture or Man

The Word of God consistently rejects new revelatory authorities.

> "But though we, or an angel from heaven, preach any other gospel unto you than that which we have preached unto you, let him be accursed."
> — Galatians 1:8

This principle applies regardless of sincerity, moral discipline, or global influence.

Once authority is relocated from Christ to a modern figure, the true gospel of Jesus Christ is altered.

---

9. Conclusion: From Visionary to Replacement Authority

The *Divine Principle*'s theology creates a vacancy that only a new messianic authority can fill. Sun Myung Moon's rise from visionary interpreter to central figure for salvation isn't an accident—it's the outcome of the system itself.

Scripture allows no such vacancy.

> "Jesus Christ the same yesterday, and today, and for ever."
> — Hebrews 13:8

Conclusion

Sun Myung Moon's authority doesn't arise from biblical warrant, but from a theological framework that first diminishes Christ's sufficiency. Once that step is taken, the rise of a new central figure becomes inevitable. The Unification Church teaches that Reverend Sun Myung Moon is the returning Messiah and that he has a special role in the spiritual realm, which includes beliefs about his ascension. Seonghwa is the transition to life in the eternal spirit world and the beginning of a new phase of ministry there. Followers view him as having completed Jesus' mission and continuing to guide them from the spiritual world.

True Christianity, however, rests on the finished work of Christ, not a continuing chain of messiahs.

CHAPTER FIVE — From “True Mother” to Sole Heir

The Expansion of Hak Ja Han Moon’s Authority

---

1. Introduction: Succession Reveals Theology

Leadership transitions expose what a movement truly believes. When authority is rooted in Christ, leadership changes don’t require doctrinal innovation truth rests in the Word of God. When authority is rooted in human figures, doctrine must adjust to preserve continuity.

The death of Sun Myung Moon in 2012 created a decisive test for Unification theology. The resulting developments reveal the internal logic of the *Divine Principle* system.

Scripture anticipates no such crisis, and God doesn’t change.

> “For I the Lord do not change; therefore you, O children of Jacob, are not consumed.”
>
> — Malachi 3:6

2. The *Divine Principle* Framework: Restoration Requires Parents

The *Divine Principle* teaches that salvation involves restoring the position of the original human ancestors.

*DP*96 states:

> "The mission of the Messiah is to restore the original position of the first human ancestors."
> — *Exposition of the Divine Principle* (1996), Part I, Chapter 7, Section 1

This framework necessarily involves **male–female pairing**, because restoration is conceived in terms of lineage rather than atonement.

*DP*96 continues:

> "The Messiah must come as the True Parent to restore fallen humanity."
> — *DP*96, Part I, Chapter 7, Section 1

From the beginning, then, Unification theology embeds the need for **human parental figures** in salvation.

---

3. Hak Ja Han Moon's Initial Role

Within the early Unification narrative, Hak Ja Han Moon's role was primarily relational rather than doctrinal. Her significance derived from her position as spouse rather than from being an independent or co-redeemer which also would imply having the power to save or redeem.

However, the *Divine Principle*'s theology already contained the seeds of later elevation: If restoration requires parents, and if those parents must be perfected, then authority cannot remain solely with one figure.

Scripture is firm on who to call Father:

> "Call no man your father upon the earth: for one is your Father, which is in heaven."
> — Matthew 23:9

4. The Succession Crisis After 2012

Sun Myung Moon's death forced a theological reckoning. If restoration depends on True Parents, what happens when one parent dies?

Rather than collapsing, the system adapted. Authority was consolidated rather than dissolved.

This development reveals that the system's authority is **not Christ-centered**, but **role-centered**.

The New Testament doesn't offer an office that requires this type of succession.

> "Wherefore he is able also to save them to the uttermost that come unto God by him, seeing he ever liveth to make intercession for them."
> —Hebrews 7:25

Christ's priesthood doesn't terminate and therefore doesn't require inheritance. He is the "Great High Priest" (Hebrews 4:14).

> "Seeing then that we have a great high priest, that is passed into the heavens, Jesus the Son of God, let us hold fast *our* profession."
>
> — Hebrews 4:14

---

5. The Emergence of Exclusive Maternal Authority

In the years following Sun Myung Moon's death, Hak Ja Han Moon's authority expanded beyond partnership into exclusivity. Claims emerged identifying her as uniquely begotten, uniquely positioned, and uniquely authoritative.

This progression isn't explained within the *Divine Principle* text itself, but it's justified through its framework. Once authority is disconnected from Scripture and grounded in lineage restoration, **roles may be redefined as needed**.

Scripture rejects this flexibility:

> "But though we, or an angel from heaven, preach any other gospel unto

> you than that which we have preached unto you, let him be accursed.
> As we said before, so say I now again, If any *man* preach any other gospel unto you than that ye have received, let him be accursed."
>
> — Galatians 1:8-9

---

6. Scripture: No Heirs Who Have the Power to Save or Redeem

The gospel recognizes no heirs that can save, no inherited offices, and no continuation of messianic authority through family lines.

> "Neither is there salvation in any other."
> — Acts 4:12

Christ's authority isn't divided, transferred, or expanded.

Paul emphasizes:

> "For in him dwelleth all the fulness of the Godhead bodily. And ye are

> complete in him which is the head of all principality and power:"
> — Colossians 2:9–10

Believers are complete in Christ—not in parental figures, lineages, or institutions.

---

7. The Pattern of Doctrinal Adaptation

The expansion of Hak Ja Han Moon's authority demonstrates a consistent pattern:

1. Christ's work is declared incomplete
2. A human role is introduced to fill the gap
3. That role becomes necessary for salvation
4. Authority adapts to preserve the system

Scripture warned against precisely this pattern:

> "For I know this, that after my departing shall grievous wolves enter in among you, not sparing the flock. Also of your own selves shall men arise, speaking perverse things, to draw away

> disciples after them."
> — Acts 20:29–30

No matter how sincere a person seems, **systemic displacement of Christ** and His rightful place as King of Kings and the only true Lord and Master is the main issue.

---

8. Gender, the Nature of Being and Salvation

The *Divine Principle*'s emphasis on male–female restoration introduces ideas about human nature that Scripture doesn't teach. Salvation becomes tied to gender roles instead of Christ's completed work.

Paul rejects such distinctions:

> "There is neither Jew nor Greek, there is neither bond nor free, there is neither male nor female: for ye are all one in Christ Jesus."
>
> — Galatians 3:28

Salvation isn't gendered. It's Christ-centered on Him alone.

---

9. Conclusion: Authority Without Biblical Anchor

Hak Ja Han Moon’s rise to sole authority is the result of a theology that:

- denies Christ’s sufficiency
- relocates salvation to lineage
- permits doctrinal evolution

Scripture allows none of these moves.

> “If ye continue in my word, then are ye my disciples indeed.”
> — John 8:31

Conclusion

The consolidation of authority in Hak Ja Han Moon reveals the instability of any system that departs from the finality of Christ. Where Christ’s work is diminished, human authority must expand to compensate.

Christianity requires no parents, and no successors, as is taught in the *Divine Principle*.

It rests entirely on the finished work of Jesus Christ, our Lord and Savior, and His Word, the Holy Bible.

CHAPTER SIX — The *Divine Principle* Examined Against Scripture

Grace, Indemnity, and the Question of Sufficiency

---

1. Introduction: The Test of Any Theology

Scripture provides a definitive standard by which all doctrine must be measured:

> "To the law and to the testimony: if they speak not according to this word, it is because there is no light in them."
> — Isaiah 8:20

Christian theology doesn't permit parallel authorities. Any system that claims compatibility with Christianity must submit entirely to what is written in the Holy Bible and the teachings of our blessed Lord and Savior, Jesus Christ.

> "I will worship toward thy holy temple, and praise thy name for thy lovingkindness and for thy truth: for thou hast magnified thy word above all thy name."

— Psalm 138:2

The *Divine Principle* presents itself as an explanatory revelation. Yet its doctrines repeatedly modify foundational biblical teachings. This chapter examines those modifications in detail.

---

2. The *Divine Principle* Doctrine of Restoration Through Indemnity

A central feature of the *Divine Principle* is the concept of **indemnity**—the idea that human beings must pay conditions to undo the effects of the Fall.

*DP*96 teaches:

> "Restoration through indemnity is the way to restore the providence of God."
> — *Exposition of the Divine Principle* (1996), Part II, Chapter 1, Section 4

Indemnity isn't presented as spiritual discipline or sanctification, but as **necessary payment** for restoration.

The text continues:

> "Man must make indemnity conditions to restore what was lost."
> — *DP*96, Part II, Chapter 1, Section 4

This framework introduces a transactional model of salvation. (Including ancestor liberation, where money is paid for liberation.)

---

3. Scripture: Salvation Is Not a Transaction

The New Testament categorically rejects any notion that salvation can be earned, paid, or balanced through human effort.

Paul writes:

> "Being justified freely by his grace through the redemption that is in Christ Jesus."
> — Romans 3:24

"Freely" (*dorean*) means **without cause or payment**.

He further states:

> "Not by works of righteousness which we have done, but according to his

> mercy he saved us."
> — Titus 3:5

Indemnity or reimbursement conditions directly contradict this teaching.

---

4. The *Divine Principle*'s "Portion of Responsibility"

Another foundational doctrine of the *Divine Principle* is the idea that God accomplishes most of salvation, but humans must fulfill a portion.

*DP*96 states:

> "God fulfills His portion of responsibility, and man fulfills his portion."
> — *DP*96, Part I, Chapter 3, Section 2

Although often framed as cooperation, this doctrine introduces **shared causation** in salvation. Scripture denies this. Christ alone paid the price.

> "For ye are bought with a price: therefore glorify God in your body, and in your spirit, which are God's."

—1 Corinthians 6:20

---

5. Scripture: God Alone Accomplishes Salvation

The Bible consistently affirms that salvation is God's work from beginning to end.

> "So then it is not of him that willeth, nor of him that runneth, but of God that sheweth mercy."
> — Romans 9:16

Jonah declared:

> "Salvation is of the LORD."
> — Jonah 2:9

The introduction of a human portion transforms grace into partnership, undermining the gospel.

---

6. Original Sin: Lineage or Moral Guilt?

The *Divine Principle* defines original sin as a **biological corruption transmitted through lineage**.

*DP*96 explains:

> "Original sin is inherited through the blood lineage of the fallen parents."
> — *DP*96, Part I, Chapter 2, Section 2

It redefines salvation as a problem of bloodline rather than a problem of sin.

---

7. Scripture: Sin Is Moral Rebellion, Not Biological

Scripture defines sin as **moral rebellion** and willful disobedience not genetic contamination.

> "The soul that sinneth, it shall die."
> — Ezekiel 18:20

Jesus taught spiritual rebirth, not bloodline purification:

> "That which is born of the flesh is flesh; and that which is born of the Spirit is spirit."
> — John 3:6

Salvation occurs through faith and accepting Jesus Christ as Lord and Savior, not genealogy.

---

8. Grace Versus Process

The *Divine Principle* presents salvation as a **historical and progressive process**, unfolding through providential stages.

*DP*96 states:

> "The providence of restoration is the providence to restore fallen man to the original ideal."
> — *DP*96, Part II, Chapter 1, Section 1

Scripture presents salvation as a **completed act** with ongoing sanctification—not a redemptive process awaiting fulfillment.

---

9. Scripture: Salvation as Present Possession

Jesus taught:

> "Verily, verily, I say unto you, He that heareth my word, and believeth on him that sent me, hath everlasting life, and shall not come into condemnation; but is passed from death unto life."
>
> — John 5:24

> ““Therefore being justified by faith, we have peace with God through our Lord Jesus Christ:”
> — Romans 5:1

Believers do not wait for salvation to become real; it becomes real when we are born again.

> “For God so loved the world, that he gave his only begotten Son, that whosoever believeth in him should not perish, but have everlasting life.”
>
> — John 3:16

---

10. The Consequence of Theological Adjustment

Each doctrinal adjustment within the *Divine Principle*—indemnity, shared responsibility, lineage-based sin—diminishes the sufficiency of Christ’s finished work.

Paul warned:

> “Christ is become of no effect unto you, whosoever of you are justified by the

> law; ye are fallen from grace."
> — Galatians 5:4

Grace and mercy cannot be earned. We can know His great love because Jesus finished the work at the cross.

> "Greater love hath no man than this, that a man lay down his life for his friends."
>
> — John 15:13

---

11. Conclusion: A System at Odds with the Gospel

The *Divine Principle* presents a different gospel. When examined against Scripture, its doctrines consistently:

- add to grace
- divide salvation
- relocate sufficiency
- require human fulfillment

Scripture allows none of these.

> "For by grace are ye saved through faith; and that not of yourselves: it is the gift of God."
> — Ephesians 2:8

Conclusion

The *Divine Principle* doesn't merely reinterpret Christian theology; it reconstructs it around principles Scripture explicitly rejects. In doing so, it presents not an explanation of the true gospel, but an alternative to it, redefining the nature of salvation and the person of Christ.

CHAPTER SEVEN — Another Spirit at Work

Discernment, Authority, and the Source of Revelation

---

1. Introduction: The Question Scripture Forces Us to Ask

Scripture never assumes that religious enthusiasm, moral discipline, or supernatural claims are automatically from God. Instead, believers are commanded to test spiritual sources.

> "Beloved, believe not every spirit, but try the spirits whether they are of God: because many false prophets are gone out into the world."
> — 1 John 4:1

The issue isn't sincerity, effort, or global influence. The issue is **source**. This chapter addresses whether the spiritual framework underlying the *Divine Principle* aligns with the teachings of Jesus Christ revealed in Scripture.

---

2. The Divine Principle's View of Revelation

The *Divine Principle* presents itself as a new and deeper revelation explaining Scripture's "hidden meaning."

*DP*96 states:

> "The Divine Principle is the truth by which we can understand the purpose of God's providence."
> — *Exposition of the Divine Principle* (1996), Introduction

Although framed as explanatory, this claim establishes a **secondary interpretive authority** that Scripture alone cannot provide.

Scripture explicitly rejects this necessity.

> "All scripture is given by inspiration of God, and is profitable for doctrine, for reproof, for correction, for instruction in righteousness: That the man of God may be perfect, throughly furnished unto all good works."
> — 2 Timothy 3:16–17

If Scripture thoroughly furnishes the believer, no supplementary revelation is required.

---

3. The Spirit Test: Confession of Christ

First John gives a decisive test for discerning spiritual sources:

> "Every spirit that confesseth that Jesus Christ is come in the flesh is of God."
> — 1 John 4:2

Confession here isn't only verbal acknowledgment, but **doctrinal fidelity** to the identity and work of Christ.

The *Divine Principle* does not affirm Jesus' incarnation and simultaneously denies the sufficiency of His completed work. He is presented as a perfected man.

*DP*96 teaches:

> "Because Jesus did not fulfill the purpose of the Messiah, the providence of restoration must continue."
> — *DP*96, Part I, Chapter 7, Section 4

This confession affirms Jesus verbally to a certain extent while denying the finality of His redemptive work, His Divinity and His Lordship.

---

4. Scripture: The Spirit of Truth Glorifies Christ, Not Replaces Him

Jesus taught that the Holy Spirit's role isn't to introduce new messianic figures, but to magnify Christ.

> "He shall glorify me: for he shall receive of mine, and shall shew it unto you."
> — John 16:14

Any spiritual system that redirects glory, loyalty, or dependence for salvation away from Christ reveals a different source.

Paul warns:

> "For Satan himself is transformed into an angel of light."
> — 2 Corinthians 11:14

False systems rarely appear hostile; sometimes they do, yet they make themselves appear to be enlightened.

---

5. The *Divine Principle*'s Spiritual Hierarchy

The *Divine Principle* describes a structured spiritual cosmos involving historical figures, eras, and graded spiritual development.

*DP*96 explains:

> "Spirits in the spirit world can cooperate with people on earth according to their level of spiritual growth."
> — *DP*96, Part II, Chapter 5

This framework creates a spiritual hierarchy that influences earthly salvation.

Scripture doesn't support this interaction as a means of salvation.

> "For there is one God, and one mediator between God and men, the man Christ

> Jesus;"
> — 1 Timothy 2:5

Any additional mediating framework violates this exclusivity. Scripture also condemns necromancy or communication with the dead.

> "There shall not be found among you any one that maketh his son or his daughter to pass through the fire, or that useth divination, or an observer of times, or an enchanter, or a witch,
> Or a charmer, or a consulter with familiar spirits, or a wizard, or a necromancer. For all that do these things are an abomination unto the LORD: and because of these abominations the LORD thy God doth drive them out from before thee."
>
> — Deuteronomy 18:10–12

---

6. Assurance Versus Anxiety

The Holy Spirit produces assurance, not perpetual striving.

> "The Spirit itself beareth witness with our spirit, that we are the children of God."
> — Romans 8:16

The *Divine Principle*, by contrast, locates assurance in continued participation, obedience, and alignment with providential figures.

This produces spiritual anxiety rather than rest.

> "Come unto me, all ye that labour and are heavy laden, and I will give you rest."
> — Matthew 11:28

Christ offers rest, not perpetual uncertainty.

---

7. The Fruit Test

Jesus provided another test:

> "Wherefore by their fruits ye shall know them."
> — Matthew 7:20

The fruit of the Spirit is clearly defined:

> "But the fruit of the Spirit is love, joy, peace, longsuffering, gentleness, goodness, faith,
> Meekness, temperance: against such there is no law."
> — Galatians 5:22–23

Systems that emphasize hierarchical obedience, fear of falling behind providence, or dependence on leadership for salvation consistently produce control rather than freedom.

---

8. Scripture: Freedom Is the Mark of the Holy Spirit

Paul declares:

> "Now the Lord is that Spirit: and where the Spirit of the Lord is, there is liberty."
> — 2 Corinthians 3:17

Freedom in Scripture doesn't mean lawlessness; it does mean complete liberation from anxiety or wondering if you're truly saved. Any system that makes you question the completed work of Jesus

Christ and asks you to keep paying contradicts the freedom that only Jesus can bring.

Any system that binds conscience to human authority contradicts this principle.

---

9. Another Spirit Defined

Paul explicitly warned the church of Corinth:

> "Ye receive another spirit, which ye have not received."
> — 2 Corinthians 11:4

This "other spirit" operates through:

- diminished work of Christ
- added revelation
- transferred authority
- redirected loyalty

The *Divine Principle* exhibits all four characteristics.

---

10. Conclusion: Testing the Spirits by the Finished Work of Christ

The test of spiritual authenticity isn't charisma, discipline, or global reach. It's fidelity to the finished work of Jesus Christ.

> "Looking unto Jesus the author and finisher of our faith; who for the joy that was set before him endured the cross, despising the shame, and is set down at the right hand of the throne of God."
> — Hebrews 12:2

If faith requires another author, another finisher, or another authority, it's no longer true Christian faith.

Conclusion

The *Divine Principle* presents itself as spiritual illumination, but when tested against Scripture, it reveals a different spirit—one that names Christ but shifts saving authority elsewhere. It isn't the Jesus of the Bible.

Scripture leaves no ambiguity:

> "If there come any unto you, and bring not this doctrine, receive him not into your house, neither bid him God speed:"
> — 2 John 1:10

Christian discernment demands no less.

APPENDIX A — *Divine Principle* Claims Index

Direct DP*96 Claims Compared with Scripture*

This index summarizes the **core doctrinal claims of the *Divine Principle***, cites where they appear in ***DP*96**, and contrasts them with **explicit Scripture**. It's intended to allow readers to verify claims directly by consulting the *DP*96 website (for reference only).

A1. Claim: Jesus Did Not Complete the Messianic Mission

***Divine Principle* (*DP*96):**

> "Jesus did not accomplish the purpose of the Messiah."
> — *DP*96, Part I, Chapter 7, Section 4

Scripture:

> "It is finished."
>
> — John 19:30
>
> "By one offering he hath perfected for ever them that are sanctified."
>
> — Hebrews 10:14

Conclusion:
Scripture explicitly declares Christ's work complete. *DP*96 denies this completion.

A2. Claim: The Crucifixion Was Not God's Original Will

***Divine Principle*:**

> "Had the Jewish people believed in Jesus, he would not have gone the way of the cross."
> — *DP*96, Part I, Chapter 4, Section 1.6

Scripture:

> "Delivered by the determinate counsel and foreknowledge of God."
>
> — Acts 2:23
>
> "Yet it pleased the LORD to bruise him."
>
> — Isaiah 53:10

Conclusion:
Scripture presents the cross as foreordained, not accidental.

A3. Claim: Salvation Is Partial (Spiritual Only)

***Divine Principle*:**

> "Jesus' crucifixion brought spiritual salvation alone."
> — *DP*96, Part I, Chapter 4, Section 1.6

Scripture:

> "Who his own self bare our sins in his own body on the tree."
>
> — 1 Peter 2:24
>
> "Greater love hath no man than this, that a man lay down his life for his friends."
>
> — John 15:13
>
> "And you, being dead in your sins and the uncircumcision of your flesh, hath he quickened together with him, having

> forgiven you all trespasses; blotting out the handwriting of ordinances that was against us, which was contrary to us, and took it out of the way, nailing it to his cross."
>
> — Colossians 2:13-14

Conclusion:
Scripture presents salvation as complete and undivided.

A4. Claim: Restoration Requires Human Indemnity

***Divine Principle*:**

> "Restoration through indemnity is the way to restore the providence of God."
> — *DP*96, Part II, Chapter 1, Section 4

Scripture:

> "Being justified freely by his grace through the redemption that is in Christ Jesus:"
>
> — Romans 3:24

> "Not by works of righteousness which we have done, but according to his mercy he saved us, by the washing of regeneration, and renewing of the Holy Ghost;"
>
> — Titus 3:5

Conclusion:
Indemnity makes human effort a necessary component of salvation, contradicting justification by grace alone.

A5. Claim: God and Man Share Responsibility for Salvation

***Divine Principle*:**

> "God fulfills His portion of responsibility, and man fulfills his portion."
> — *DP*96, Part I, Chapter 3, Section 2

Scripture:

> "Salvation is of the LORD."
>
> — Jonah 2:9

> "It is not of him that willeth."
>
> — Romans 9:16

Conclusion:
Scripture attributes salvation solely to God.

A6. Claim: Original Sin Is Lineage-Based

***Divine Principle*:**

> "Original sin is inherited through the blood lineage."
> — *DP*96, Part I, Chapter 2, Section 2

Scripture:

> "The soul that sinneth, it shall die. The son shall not bear the iniquity of the father, neither shall the father bear the iniquity of the son: the righteousness of the righteous shall be upon him, and the wickedness of the wicked shall be upon him."
>
> — Ezekiel 18:20

> "But as many as received him, to them gave he power to become the sons of God, even to them that believe on his name: Which were born, not of blood, nor of the will of the flesh, nor of the will of man, but of God."
>
> — John 1:12-13

Conclusion:
Scripture defines sin as willful disobedience, not biological corruption.

A7. Claim: A New Messiah Must Complete Restoration

***Divine Principle*:**

> "The Messiah must come again… to complete the providence of restoration."
> — *DP*96, Part I, Chapter 7, Section 4

Scripture:

> "For *there is* one God, and one mediator between God and men, the man Christ Jesus;"
>
> —1 Timothy 2:5

Conclusion:
Scripture allows no replacement or supplementary Messiah.

APPENDIX B — Chronology of Messianic Claims in Unification Theology

This chronology traces **doctrinal development**, not personal biography.

1935 — Vision Narrative of Sun Myung Moon

Claimed encounter with Jesus assigning a mission. **Significance:** Establishes private revelation as authority. "Jesus appeared before me and asked me to accomplish the mission left unfulfilled by him."

1954 — Founding of the Unification Church

Institutional vehicle for *Divine Principle* theology.

1960 — "True Parents" Doctrine Introduced

Marriage framed as cosmic restoration event.

1960s–1970s — Central Figure Emphasis

Moon increasingly described as indispensable to God's providence.

1980s — Global Political and Interfaith Engagement

Messianic authority linked to world peace initiatives.

1990s — Explicit Second Advent Teaching

Internal doctrine identifies Moon as "Lord of the Second Advent."

2000s — Expanded Providential Claims

Messianic authority tied to global reconciliation efforts.

2012 — Death of Sun Myung Moon

Triggers doctrinal succession crisis.

2013–2018 — Authority Reframed

Hak Ja Han Moon elevated as central redemptive authority.

Late 2010s — "Only Begotten Daughter" Claim

Authority consolidated exclusively in Hak Ja Han Moon.

APPENDIX C — Public Figures and Religious Leaders Associated with Unification-Linked Events

Editorial Note:

Inclusion documents **participation**, not necessarily endorsement of theology.

C1. Christian Pastors and Evangelical Leaders

- Paula White-Cain
- Mark Burns
- Bishop Noel Jones
- Archbishop George Augustus Stallings Jr.
- Various Pentecostal and Charismatic pastors at UPF/Rally of Hope events

---

C2. Gospel Singers and Musical Participants

- BeBe Winans
- CeCe Winans
- Yolanda Adams
- Donnie McClurkin

- Little Angels Folk Ballet of Korea

C3. Political Figures and Heads of State

- Donald J. Trump
- Mike Pence
- Mike Pompeo
- Newt Gingrich
- Dan Burton
- George H. W. Bush
- Barbara Bush
- Ban Ki-moon
- Hun Sen

C4. Interfaith Participants

- Rabbis participating in UPF peace forums
- Muslim clerics at interfaith summits

- Catholic and Orthodox representatives at unity events

Appendix C: Editorial Purpose

This appendix demonstrates **how legitimacy is constructed** through association, not doctrinal agreement.

APPENDIX C (EXPANDED)

Christian Pastors, Gospel Artists, Religious Leaders, and Political Figures Appearing at Events Sponsored or Co-Sponsored by Unification-Affiliated Organizations

The following lists document **reported participation or appearances** at events sponsored, co-sponsored, or organized by Unification-affiliated organizations (including the Universal Peace Federation, Rally of Hope, World Summit series, and related initiatives).

Inclusion doesn't imply theological agreement, endorsement of Unification doctrine, or ongoing affiliation.

Readers are encouraged to consult event programs, video recordings, and official announcements to evaluate context and content for themselves. My conclusion is that Christians shouldn't participate.

> "And have no fellowship with the unfruitful works of darkness, but rather reprove *them*."
>
> — Ephesians 5:11

C1. Christian Pastors and Evangelical Leaders

These individuals have appeared as **speakers, prayer leaders, panelists, or guests** at Unification-affiliated peace, prayer, or unity events.

- **Paula White-Cain**
  Participated in prayer or speaking roles at interfaith or unity events connected with UPF/Rally of Hope initiatives.

- **Mark Burns**
  Appeared at faith-based or prayer events associated with Unification-linked peace gatherings.

- **Bishop Noel Jones**
  Participated in interfaith or peace-oriented events connected with UPF-sponsored programs.

- **Archbishop George Augustus Stallings Jr.**
  Long-standing public participant, served as speaker and emcee at multiple Unification-linked events over several years.

- **Various Pentecostal and Charismatic Pastors**
  Appeared as local clergy representatives, prayer leaders, or panel participants at **Rally of Hope** events in the United States and internationally.

C2. Gospel Singers and Christian Musical Artists

These artists have appeared as **musical guests or performers** at events sponsored or co-sponsored by Unification-affiliated organizations.

- **BeBe Winans**
  Gospel performer at peace, unity, or faith-based events associated with Unification sponsors.
- **CeCe Winans**
  Participated as a musical guest at interfaith or unity gatherings connected to UPF or Rally of Hope programming.
- **Yolanda Adams**
  Featured gospel artist at peace-oriented events with Unification-linked sponsorship.
- **Donnie McClurkin**
  Gospel performer at faith-based events connected with Unification-affiliated peace initiatives.
- **Little Angels Folk Ballet of Korea**
  Cultural performance group founded under Unification auspices, frequently featured at

World Summits and peace events as a cultural ambassador ensemble.

C3. Christian Leaders from Other Traditions

These individuals appeared in **interfaith or ecumenical contexts** at Unification-linked events.

- Catholic, Orthodox, and Protestant clergy participating in prayer panels or peace discussions
- Christian leaders from non-Pentecostal traditions invited to represent broader Christian unity initiatives

---

C4. Political Figures and Government Leaders (United States)

These individuals appeared as **speakers, video contributors, or honored guests** at Unification-affiliated summits or events.

- **President Donald J. Trump**
  Delivered a video address to a UPF World Summit.

- **Mike Pence**
  Appeared as a speaker at a UPF-affiliated World Summit event.

- **George H. W. Bush**
  Participated as a speaker at a Unification-linked event in the 1990s.

- **Barbara Bush**
  Appeared alongside George H. W. Bush at Unification-associated events.

C5. International Political Figures

- **Ban Ki-moon, Former UN Secretary General**
  Served as chair or senior figure in Think Tank 2022, a UPF-connected initiative.

- **Hun Sen, Former Prime Minister of Cambodia**

Associated with UPF-sponsored peace summits in Cambodia.

- Former heads of state and parliamentary leaders
  Participated in World Summit and peace-forum programming sponsored by Unification-affiliated organizations.

C6. Interfaith Religious Leaders

- Rabbis participating in UPF peace forums
- Muslim imams and scholars appearing at interfaith summits
- Buddhist and other religious representatives at World Summit events

These appearances were typically framed as **dialogue and peacebuilding**.

C7. Purpose of Documentation

This appendix serves to illustrate **how public legitimacy is constructed** through association with respected figures across religion, culture, and politics.

The appendix does the following:
- document public participation
- encourage transparency
- invite readers to compare public presentation with internal doctrine examined in this book.

PHOTO SECTION

Public-Domain Images

Photo Credits and Rights Notice

All images included in this section are believed to be in the public domain or used under conditions appropriate for publication (public-domain sources, official government images, archival materials, or rights-cleared reproductions).

Where possible, original sources and access dates are provided.
If any rights holder believes an image has been used in error, the publisher will promptly review and correct the matter in future printings.

This section is intended to **document publicly verifiable figures and events**, not to imply endorsement or affiliation beyond what is shown.

Sun Myung Moon Meeting President Richard Nixon at the White House, 1974

Sun Myung Moon meets President Richard Nixon at the White House, February 1974. Public domain White House photograph (U.S. government work)

Sun Myung Moon with Hak Ja Han

Sun Myung Moon and Hak Ja Han at a public event.

Photo licensed under CC BY-SA 3.0 via Wikimedia Commons.

Donald J. Trump and Paula White- Cain at the White House

President Donald J. Trump and Pastor Paula White at a White House event. Both have participated in programs connected to the Universal Peace Federation.
Public domain White House photograph

Vice President Mike Pence

Former Vice President Mike Pence served as the 48th Vice President of the United States from 2017 to 2021. Pence later appeared as a speaker at events affiliated with the Universal Peace Federation.

Public domain U.S. government photograph

Yolanda Adams Sings at the White House, 2007

Yolanda Adams performing at the White House, February 11, 2007. She also participated as a speaker at programs affiliated with events hosted by Sun Myung Moon and the Universal Peace Federation.

Public domain U.S. government photograph

Former Speaker of the House Newt Gingrich

Official congressional portrait of Newt Gingrich: Gingrich has participated as a speaker at events affiliated with the Universal Peace Federation, an organization founded by Sun Myung Moon. Public domain U.S. Government photograph

Former Congressman Dan Burton

Former U.S. Representative from Indiana, Burton has appeared at events associated with the Universal Peace Federation.
Public domain U.S. Government photograph

Shinzo Abe

Shinzo Abe: Former Prime Minister of Japan. Abe delivered a recorded address to a 2021 event hosted by the Universal Peace Federation, founded by Sun Myung Moon.
Public domain Government of Japan photograph (assassinated 2022)

Prayer to be Born Again and to Receive Jesus Christ as Your Lord and Savior:

Dear Lord Jesus, I know that I am a sinner, and I ask for Your forgiveness. I believe You died for my sins and rose from the dead. I trust and follow You as my Lord and Savior. Take my life and help me to do Your will. In Jesus' name, amen.

> "That if thou shalt confess with thy mouth the Lord Jesus, and shalt believe in thine heart that God hath raised him from the dead, thou shalt be saved."
>
> — Romans 10:9
>
> "For God so loved the world, that he gave his 'only' begotten Son, that whosoever believeth in him should not perish, but have everlasting life. For God sent not his Son into the world to condemn the world; but that the world through him might be saved."
>
> — John 3:16-17
>
> "For by grace are ye saved through faith; and that not of yourselves: it is the

gift of God: Not of works, lest any man should boast. "

— Ephesians 2:8-9

"Neither is there salvation in any other: for there is none other name under heaven given among men, whereby we must be saved."

— Acts 4:12

APPENDIX D — Documentary Citations from *Exposition of the Divine Principle* (1996 English Edition)

Editorial Statement

The following citations are drawn from the 1996 English edition of *Exposition of the Divine Principle* (*DP*96). References are provided by Part, Chapter, and Section to facilitate direct verification within the official text.

Primary source:
https://www.unification.net/dp96/

D1. Jesus' Mission and the Necessity of the Second Advent

"Jesus, knowing that the redemption by the cross would not completely fulfill the purpose for which he came, promised he would come again."
— *Exposition of the Divine Principle* (1996), Part I, Chapter 7, Section 4

"Similarly, the purpose of Christ at the Second Advent is to build a new heaven and a new earth upon the foundation of the spiritual salvation which had been laid by Christianity in the New Testament Age. When he returns, he will not merely repeat the words of the New Testament given two thousand years ago, but will surely add new words of truth necessary for the founding of a new heaven and a new earth. However, those Christians of today whose minds are narrowly attached to the letter of the New Testament will criticize the words and deeds of Christ at his return based on their narrow understanding of the Scriptures. Therefore, it can be expected that they will brand the Lord a heretic and persecute him. This is why Jesus foretold that at the Second Advent, Christ would first suffer many things and be rejected by his generation."

—*Exposition of the Divine Principle* (1996),

Part I, Chapter 7, Section 4

In Unification theology, the "Christ at the Second Advent" referred to here is understood to be **Sun Myung Moon**, who is believed to bring the additional truth necessary to complete the work that Jesus began.

D2. Salvation Through the Cross

Still, difficult issues remain. Christians believe that salvation is given through the atonement of the cross. Yet no one has ever given birth to a child who is sinless and in no need of redemption by the Savior.

— *Exposition of the Divine Principle* (1996), Introduction, p. 23.

D3. Original Sin and Lineage

"...Christians have been engrafted with Jesus only spiritually. This is why the children of even the most devout Christian parents still inherit sin, which must be redeemed."
— *Exposition of the Divine Principle* (1996), Part I, Chapter 2, Section 2

D4. The Second Advent

"Jesus is to come again at the close of the New Testament Age."
— *Exposition of the Divine Principle* (1996), Part I, Chapter 3, Section 2.3

D5. Restoration and Historical Providence

"Since the Fall, God has been repeatedly working His providence to restore the Kingdom."
— *Exposition of the Divine Principle* (1996), Part I, Chapter 4, Introduction

Concluding Note:

Readers can consult the full 1996 edition of *Exposition of the Divine Principle* for extended context surrounding these doctrinal statements (for research purposes only).

APPENDIX E — Documentary citations on "Only Begotten Daughter," "Original Sin," "Substantial Holy Spirit," "Bride," and the Messiah

(excerpts from Hak Ja Han speeches, *DP*96, and Unification canonical compilations)

Editorial statement:
The following excerpts are drawn from (1) speeches attributed to Hak Ja Han and archived at tparents.org, (2) the 1996 English edition of *Exposition of the Divine Principle* (*DP*96), and (3) Unification canonical compilations (e.g., Chambumo Gyeong; Cheon Seong Gyeong 2014). References are provided for verification. These excerpts are presented with and without commentary.

Primary archive sources:
https://www.tparents.org/
https://www.unification.net/dp96/

E1. "Only Begotten Daughter" (Hak Ja Han)

"The only begotten Daughter of God, whom Heaven had lost, was finally born…"

— Hak Ja Han, July 25, 2019 (tparents.org, HakJaHan-190725)

In Unification theology, this statement means that Hak Ja Han is understood to be the providentially restored "only begotten Daughter" — a sinless Eve figure whom Heaven had intended from the beginning, but who was "lost" at the Fall and is now believed to have appeared in history.

"I was the first to announce, 'I am the only begotten Daughter of God'..."
— Hak Ja Han, July 25, 2019 (tparents.org, HakJaHan-190725)

E2. "Born Without/Unrelated to Original Sin" (Hak Ja Han)

"Heaven... establish[ed] the only begotten daughter... who had nothing to do with original sin..."
— Hak Ja Han, October 6, 2016 (tparents.org, HakJaHan-161006c)

"Jesus Christ came as the only begotten son... Heaven's lineage, unrelated to

Satan…"
— Hak Ja Han, October 6, 2016 (tparents.org, HakJaHan-161006c)

E3. "Substantial Holy Spirit" + "Only Begotten Daughter" (Hak Ja Han)

"Jesus Christ and the substantial Holy Spirit, the only begotten Daughter, are both here."

"As at the time of Pentecost, the substantial Holy Spirit and only begotten Daughter has now come…"
— Hak Ja Han, May 19, 2024, Munich (tparents.org, HakJaHan-240519a)

E4. "Only Begotten Daughter" + "True Mother" (Hak Ja Han)

"As the only begotten Daughter and True Mother…"
— Hak Ja Han, July 18, 2024 (tparents.org, HakJaHan-240718)

"Welcoming Assembly… Our True Mother, the Substantial Holy Spirit and Only Begotten Daughter"

— Event title within the July 18, 2024, document (tparents.org, HakJaHan-240718)

E5. “Bride” + “Second Advent” + “True Parents” (Hak Ja Han)

“The Lord has found his bride, God’s only-begotten daughter, and they have manifested as the True Parents.”
— Hak Ja Han, August 12, 2014 (tparents.org, HakJaHan-140812)

E6. Holy Spirit as “True Mother/Second Eve” (*DP*96)

“There must be a True Mother… The Holy Spirit came as the True Mother.”
— *Exposition of the Divine Principle* (1996), Part I, Chapter 7 (“Christology”)

“The Holy Spirit comes as the True Mother, the second Eve.”
— *Exposition of the Divine Principle* (1996), Part I, Chapter 7 (“Christology”)

E7. Bride/Bride’s Language Connected to Holy Spirit (*DP*96)

"Without first receiving her, we cannot go before Jesus as his brides."
— *Exposition of the Divine Principle* (1996), Part I, Chapter 7 ("Christology")

E8. Holy Spirit "in the Flesh"/"Actual Woman"/Jesus as Bridegroom (*Chambumo Gyeong*)

"The Holy Spirit is the True Mother of humankind. Therefore, the Holy Spirit must come to the earth in the flesh."
— *Chambumo Gyeong*, Book 1 (tparents.org, ChambumoGyeong-01)

"In the beginning… the Holy Spirit, a feminine spirit, must come to earth as an actual woman…"
— *Chambumo Gyeong*, Book 1 (tparents.org, ChambumoGyeong-01)

"This will happen when Jesus comes again… as the Bridegroom…"
— *Chambumo Gyeong*, Book 1 (tparents.org, ChambumoGyeong-01)

(In Unification theology, this refers **not to the historic Christian Jesus returning in the traditional sense**, but to the **Lord of the Second Advent, Sun Myung Moon). Jesus isn't eternal God — He is the first perfected human in their view.**

E9. "Only Daughter" Requirement + "Lord at the Second Advent" as "Only Son" (Chambumo Gyeong)

"It is an original requirement that True Mother must be the only Daughter."
— *Chambumo Gyeong*, Book 2 (tparents.org, ChambumoGyeong-02)

"Jesus was the only Son. The Lord at the Second Advent is also the only Son…"
— *Chambumo Gyeong*, Book 2 (tparents.org, ChambumoGyeong-02)

E10. "True Parents," the Messiah, and the Second Advent

— *Cheon Seong Gyeong* (2014), Book 2

"The Messiah means the True Parents. They are the final destination of human history."

— *Cheon Seong Gyeong* (2014), Book 2, Chapter 1, Section 1 (202-348, 1990.05.27)

"What is the purpose of the Second Advent? It is the coming of the True Parents. The returning Lord and his bride are the True Parents."
— *Cheon Seong Gyeong* (2014), Book 2, Chapter 1, Section 1 (202-348, 1990.05.27)

"Jesus was unable to become the True Parent due to the disbelief of the people. … This means that the Lord of the Second Advent must restore the position of the Parents, spiritually and physically."
— *Cheon Seong Gyeong* (2014), Book 2, Chapter 1, Section 2 (13-283, 1964.04.12)

Chambumo Gyeong is an official scripture compilation of speeches by **Sun Myung Moon**, published by the Family Federation after his death. The title means "Scripture of the True Parents."

It's organized into multiple "Books" (major sections). **Book 2** is the second section within the larger volume and focuses on themes such as the providence of restoration, the identity and mission of True Parents, the Lord of the Second Advent, and the Only Son/Only Daughter framework. It's not a separate publication, but part of the larger canonical text used within the movement.

Commentary: In Unification theology as presented in ***Exposition of the Divine Principle***, the term **"substantial"** means embodied or physically manifested rather than merely spiritual. **Jesus** is understood as the Second Adam who accomplished spiritual salvation through the cross, but didn't establish a physical, sinless family.

The **Messiah at the Second Advent** is identified with **Sun Myung Moon**, who is regarded as the **Third Adam**, coming to complete the restoration left unfinished at Jesus' first coming by establishing a sinless lineage.

The **Bride** isn't symbolic, but a literal woman who stands in the restored Eve position; this role is identified with **Hak Ja Han Moon** as True Mother, and in later teachings, she is described as the "substantial" (embodied) fulfillment of the feminine Holy Spirit role within the providence of restoration.

My prayer for all who adhere to Unification theology and are members of the Family Federation is that they will come to know the truth that can only be found in the One that truly loves you, the spotless sinless Lamb of God, our precious Lord and one "true" Savior Jesus Christ. Amen.

> "And I saw heaven opened, and behold a white horse; and he that sat upon him *was* called Faithful and "True" and in righteousness he doth judge and make war."
>
> —Revelation 19:11

www.ingramcontent.com/pod-product-compliance
Lightning Source LLC
LaVergne TN
LVHW010104110826
845155LV00028B/479